Relationship Marketing³

The Ground Game for Small Business Success

Martin Brossman & Pat Howlett

Cedar Books

Testimonials from Clients and Readers

I have been fortunate enough to know and work with both Martin and Pat for years. These two are the ultimate connectors. They live it every day and teach it in every way.

Collected in this book are some brilliant concepts you can apply today, wherever you are, to drive referrals so that they become second nature.

Their actions remind me of this quote: "Help others achieve their dreams and you will achieve yours." – Les Brown

All the best!

Stephen Hand
BNI Executive Director, NC Triangle and NC Coastal

***

I just reviewed Martin's book that he co-authored with Pat Howlett called *Relationship Marketing to the 3rd Power*. In the book, they explain how word-of-mouth by satisfied clients and customers is worth its weight in gold, but you must provide great service and also follow their process for the best results.

Dana Gower

***

My name is Deborah Hoover; I'm with *Spotted Dots*. What I got out of Martin Brossman's "Relationship Marketing" class is that you really are able to grow your business, and mine has grown. It's actually doubled within these six months!

So, I encourage everyone to take it (Relationship Marketing), mainly because I was able to promote my customers and they were able to promote me. Thus, it's kind of a win-win scenario. I could gain more momentum in my business just from the simple ways of asking for referrals. Now, there's a specific process that needs to be taken care of. And in the "Relationship Marketing" class, I was able to learn how to do that very carefully, in the correct way.

Deborah Hoover
Spotted Dots

Acknowledgments

First, I want to thank all the owners of small businesses, clients and participants who have added to my life over the years -- and who have helped Pat and me by applying our principles and gaining success from them. Special kudos to our Junto, BBB, for their support.

Next, I want to express my gratitude to Jane Maulucci who transcribed this training program into a well-written, entertaining document. If you have ever attempted to transcribe lengthy, audio-recorded conversations into text, you know the amazing amount of ability and patience it requires. Jane Maulucci has so many skills. Among others, she is a talented writer, an audiobook narrator, and a networking champion of the small business community.

Finally, I would also like to thank the following: Colleen Gray and Beth Zecca, who successfully support my company, Martin Brossman & Associates. My wife and the love of my, Barbara Carr Brossman, who inspires me to be a better man each day and enhances my best ideas. My stepson, Emery Carr, who is a brilliant, Senior Data Scientist, deep thinker, and creative genius with whom I often bounce ideas. My "Technology Sharing Team" that has met once a week for many years. And my best friend and the publisher of this book, Richard Grassi.

Martin Brossman

I'd like to acknowledge the inside919 Community. You were the reason this content was originally created, and you all proved that it works. Thank you so much!

Pat Howlett

CONTENTS

CHAPTER 1

YOU ALREADY DO IT

"The secret to marketing success is no secret at all: Word
of mouth is all that matters."
Seth Godin, Founder and CEO, Do You Zoom

What happens when you find a product, service, or experience that you really enjoy? You tell people about it. And when a family member, friend, colleague, or even a stranger asks you for a recommendation, your eyes light up, and you tell them where to find the best food, music, or orthopedist. That's word-of-mouth marketing and, in our opinion, the best type of marketing you can get.

It is highly cost-effective because people who have experienced a product or service endorse it and put their reputation behind it to encourage others to participate. Their words have weight. Their opinion is valued and trusted. Simply put, Relationship Marketing is the next-level word of mouth.

We aim to give you a system to consistently use Relationship Marketing to build your business. Once you have the system in place, you'll find that you can grow your business exponentially and work with people who are exactly the clients you want to work with, people who recognize your value and are willing and able to pay for it.

This systematic approach is reciprocal and requires you to be willing to refer businesses you know, like, and trust to others. As a result, you'll learn to do business better and create a network of like-minded colleagues who keep each other top of mind and on the lookout for opportunities to refer and partner together.

Referrals Offer the Best Rate of Return

The client that comes to you on a referral isn't buying based on price. They are willing to work with you because they trust the person who referred them to you. You get what we call "third-party validation" or "borrowed reputation."

After establishing your Relationship Marketing System, prospects sent your way are also more qualified because your referral partner knows enough about your business to clearly convey what you offer and your value.

Build Your Ground Game First

We know social media is important in building your business and developing top-of-mind awareness. But *likes* don't buy things; people do. Your ground game is what you do offline to connect with real live people. It is having a cup of coffee (even virtually) with a colleague and getting to know them and their business. By learning what they need and how you can help them grow, you will start to expand your network, which is the foundation of your business and your Relationship Marketing System. We'll walk you through the process in later chapters.

Understand that this personal and local connection is something that big businesses can't offer. Most local business owners and service providers make the majority of their money within about five miles of where they live. They want to support each other and their community. They understand that all boats rise on a high tide. We're giving you the way to encourage the tide to rise.

It Works When You're Not There

Imagine you're on a Zoom call, ready to introduce yourself to the group, and suddenly your computer freezes. This happened in one of Martin's technical classes. Fortunately, Martin knew the person and their business well enough that he could give them a fantastic introduction. Not only did Martin serve his colleague well, but everyone on the call was impressed that he had taken the time to get to know someone and to endorse them so enthusiastically. It made the participants want to have that type of connection which they can with Relationship Marketing.

Know What You Do and Who You Serve

Before anyone can recommend you and your business, you must be absolutely clear about what you can deliver and your ideal client. This ensures that you will provide the best service and solutions to the people who really appreciate you (and refer you to others) while avoiding the customers or clients you can't satisfy. This clarity also means that you can be specific when reaching out to referral partners so they can stand in for you, as Martin did, and promote you properly.

Relationship Marketing is personal and reciprocal. You are putting your knowledge and reputation on the line to support a business connection, just as they would for you. You'll have a consistent flow of opportunities to give and receive when you systematize it.

CHAPTER 2

TAKING CONTROL OF WORD OF MOUTH ADVERTISING

"Do what you do so well that people can't resist telling
others about you."
Walt Disney

Most folks agree that word-of-mouth advertising is the best way
to market. Relationship Marketing is structured word of mouth that
you carefully control. You control the message and the messenger to
attract the people you want to work with. These people recognize the
value of your products and services and are excited to rely on your
expertise.

If you have a problem considering yourself an expert, take a moment to
understand that you have knowledge and experience that your potential
clients don't have. That is enough to make you an expert. With that in

mind, take the next step and start thinking about how you want to be known.

Define Your Expertise

Imagine you are a real estate agent. Your expertise may be working with first-time buyers, downsizing empty nesters, or selling historic homes. Each buying situation requires a different skill set and approach, each with its own target market. Without defining your expertise, you will get referrals you don't want and can't truly serve appropriately.

Take the time to think about your ideal client and create their customer persona to know precisely who you are looking for and how you are the expert for them. Once you have their customer persona, you can develop your *Positioning Statement* so that when someone asks, "What do you do?" you have a clearly defined and memorable answer.

- I guide first-time buyers through the process of finding their just right first home.

- I specialize in transitioning retirees and empty nesters to a more comfortable nest.

- I focus on marketing homes that are in historic districts.

All three of these people are real estate agents, and each one of them is an expert for a different target market. These answers quickly identify their expertise, who they serve as well as who they don't serve.

You must give your referral partners a complete picture of what you do and who you serve to get referrals. These referral partners are friends, family, colleagues, and others in your network or circle of influence.

Notice that the word "network" has "work" in it. As you can tell, this system goes beyond wishing and hoping you stumble across someone who knows someone who needs you and that this person will hand out your card for you. Relationship Marketing is a planned and thoughtful process. You have to work at it.

Reviews are Relationship Marketing

Word of mouth also travels by social media. Whichever platform you use, you want to have positive, heartfelt reviews from your customers that support your expertise.

Imagine you are looking at a book on Amazon. After the title and the summary, you go to the reviews to see if you want to commit yourself to purchasing and reading the book. If the reader reviews are mostly five stars and submitted by people who don't seem to be related to the author, you are more likely to put that book in your cart. You have confidence that this book is worth it because of the reviews.

As part of your Relationship Marketing Strategy (RMS), build online reviews for your business. Ask your customers or clients to submit a review on social media or a testimonial for your website. If they send you an email or note raving about your products and services, then reach out, thank them, and ask if you could quote them on your website if they aren't social media savvy.

With these two steps, your foundation is in place, and you are now managing your word of mouth. You have clarified what you do and who you serve, and you are actively asking for reviews from your delighted customers. Your next step is to get an active and continuous flow of referrals.

Receiving Referrals

Now referrals are starting to come in because you have clarified your expertise, and people know, like, and trust you. The referrals are the first product from your RMS machine, and you must handle each one carefully.

Here's the scenario: Pat is talking to Chris, who says she needs a business coach to help her better understand her social media marketing strategy. Pat tells Chris that Martin is the guy who can guide her and provides the contact information. A few days later, Chris reaches out to Martin and initiates the first step of his RMS – he makes Pat look good.

Martin will extol Pat's virtues as a business person and a human to Chris. His praise reinforces that Pat is a person of value and that this referral is appreciated. Immediately after this initial meeting, Martin will call Pat and thank him for the referral even if Chris decides not to work with Martin.

Pat certainly deserves the gratitude, and Martin is happy to give it. However, Pat also needs to know whether the referral goes well or not. If it went well, Pat knows that he fully understands Martin's target market and correctly matches Chris' needs to Martin's solution.

If it didn't go well, Pat needs to know if he misrepresented Martin or if Chris wasn't a good fit for some reason to be confident about the people he refers to in the future.

You may think that a responsive phone call is not much of a thank you for Pat's referral. The truth is that Martin knows Pat and his business well enough that Martin is part of Pat's RMS machine. So along with his gratitude, Martin will be sending appropriate referrals to Pat.

Handling the Prospect

During the first contact with your referred prospect and after making your referral partner look good, you find out what the prospect needs. This is not the time to pitch your products or services; this is when you ask questions to uncover their problem to determine if you have the solution.

If you are not a good fit for them, consider who else in your collection of strategic partners or other businesses would be a better match and refer them to that person.

If you clearly see you can help them, let them know you would love to work with them. We don't "close" deals. Instead, we invite people to work with us. We explain our process and carefully review everything you are willing to offer them. Then you ask if you provide everything as promised, will they *refer you to three people in 90 days*?

We can hear you already balking at using such a strong statement, "I won't ever do that. I only ask for referrals at the very end when I've already done things. So now you're telling me I need to say these things when I first meet people at the very beginning?"

Yes, that's what we're saying. You're going to resist, there's going to be some pushback, and we're going to say the best way to get around that is to remember that you are a professional. Your products and services are valuable.

You're going to do a value exchange with people where you exchange what you give them for money. You do such a good job that they will *want* to provide you with referrals. You have to expect referrals. A referral is how they came to you, and they have witnessed the ease and success of the process.

Most potential clients are happy to comply with your request, and the ones who will not agree are not a fit for your business. If they object to this, you should expect they will also be challenging in other aspects. Remember, you get to choose who you work with.

The Ask

Once you have established the high value you bring to your clients, you'll find asking for the referrals upfront is almost painless. This new behavior takes practice in a safe environment before you feel confident. You can practice asking for referrals with friends, colleagues, or your favorite mirror. The more comfortable you are with the referral request, the easier it will be.

Keep it simple. Explain your process and the value you bring to your clients, and confirm the deadlines.

Here's our hypothetical landscapers' introduction: "At Brossman & Howlett Landscaping, we are 'the always on time, no-mess ever left behind, and we even-make-your-neighbors happy landscaper'. Our business is based solely on referrals, and we are certain that you will be so satisfied with our services that we ask you to refer three new people to our business within 90 days."

At the beginning of his training sessions for the North Carolina Small Business Centers, Martin says, "I asked about your businesses and your goals so I can customize this class for you. My business is based on referrals. I can work on referrals because I will give you so much value in this seminar that, in return, I ask you to bring three new people with you the next time you attend one of my sessions. I am confident I will provide the value I promised, and you'll be happy to bring those three people to my class next month."

Ask fearlessly, back it up with your actions, and those referrals will pour in.

Integrity

When you recommend one of your colleagues, understand that your reputation is on the line. For example, Martin had an instance where he was co-teaching a course with a website designer, *Will Don't (WD)*. After the class, Seymour, one of the participants, hired the designer to build their new website. Seymour also paid WD $600 upfront.

WD did not respond to Seymour after accepting the job and the cash and made no attempts to communicate. Finally, in frustration, Seymour reached out to Martin and explained the situation.

Martin intervened because his reputation was on the line just as much as WD's. When Martin learned that WD couldn't do the job, he found someone else who could. He arranged with another website wizard to build the site, paid him $600 (lower than his usual site build rate), and agreed to send referrals to him in the future. The wizard recognized the value of being part of Martin's network and happily agreed.

Martin pulled the funds out of his own pocket to pay for Seymour's website and finally connected with WD. Martin conveyed his disappointment; WD apologized and then spent the next two years earning back his good reputation and providing Martin with website services, *pro bono*.

Martin didn't have to jump in and save Seymour's website. He did it because he had silently endorsed WD by standing next to him in the classroom as part of his team. Martin preserved his authority and reputation by showing the integrity to stand behind his referrals or make things right.

When you are recommending colleagues, know that your reputation goes with them. So be sure that is something you want them to carry and protect for you.

Chapter 3

Develop the Mindset

"Satisfied customers who will spread word of mouth are the
most powerful assets you have."
Andy Sernovit

The biggest obstacle to success in relationship marketing is in your head.
If you don't think you have the best solution for the people you serve, you
are defeated before you begin.

You are Worthy

Imagine Wendy, the landscaper, with a fleet of little trucks that service
residential clients. Unfortunately, Wendy believes that referrals are out
of reach for her until she has a large hauling truck emblazoned with her
company name and logo.

It's not true. It is not the truck holding Wendy back; it's her mindset. As she is, Wendy can be a referral partner with nurseries, hardware stores, senior services, and realtors, to name a few. Plus, she has a list of extremely satisfied customers. So by giving and getting referrals, she could have her truck in no time!

If Wendy is sure that the truck will make a difference in her business, she should look in her referral network for truck dealers and bankers who can help her get it. However, if you're not feeling competent because you are missing a credential, go get it. If your phone service is lousy or your office staff is sub-par, then fix it. *Never allow the things you can control to keep you from success.* Go back to your network and ask for referrals to find your solutions.

Be Consistent

To be proficient at using your Relationship Marketing Strategy (RMS), you've got to follow a structured process and be mindful of it at all times. Stay alert and listen to the needs and wants of your connections, learn more about their businesses, and be ready to give and get referrals.

Unfortunately, some people push back at the idea of a structured system, fearing it will sound canned, rehearsed, and impersonal. However, once you are comfortable clearly stating your value and asking for the three referrals, you'll find it as simple as breathing. You'll do it without stopping to think about it. It will become your mindset.

By establishing this RMS with every client, you are setting expectations for them and yourself. With this process, you are interviewing them to see if they are a good fit. Then, by telling them, "I'm going to make you so happy that you did business with me that you're going to refer three new clients to me in the next 90 days. In fact, that is exactly how I grow my business."

You have to mean it and believe it when you say it. That's part of the RMS Mindset. Of course, your potential client will be stunned by such a statement, but you'll know if they will be worth your effort by their response.

Use your RMS positioning statement to establish the expectations with every client. This statement is like a lighthouse drawing in the right ships to your safe harbor. It also culls the potentially troublesome client but leaves them feeling very positive about you. Their word of mouth could lead to a new contact.

Pat notes that while he is in the marketing business, he doesn't do ads. Instead, his business is 100% referral-based from businesses, agencies, and internal marketing departments. That's how he knows this RMS mindset works. It is the anchor of his marketing plan.

To be clear, not everyone will refer three people within 90 days, and maybe not ever. That's because we are dealing with humans, and life happens, and we all get busy.

Understand that you are not asking for referrals. You are setting the expectation that they will reward you with the three referrals when you deliver as promised. You are establishing a condition for doing business with you.

If your potential client says they prefer not to give the referrals, you can choose not to work with them. It might sound drastic, but look at what you potentially lose. You'll be working with someone who does not share your business ideals. They will most likely be very demanding and unless you double your price, the job won't be worth your time and aggravation.

The RMS mindset allows you to select your clients while expanding your business.

Finding Referrals

Three key sources for finding referrals are your current clients, referral networks, and your circle of influence. You should have no problem pulling out valuable clients and projects by engaging with these three resources. So, in the next 30 days, do your research and build your mutually beneficial network.

Clients

If you've been in business for a while, you have a client list of people who spent money with you and enjoyed the process and the outcome. You got them a solution for their problem.

Reach out to them and ignite that connection-spark again. Remind your happy clients of your work and ask them if they know of anyone who might need your services. Give them your RMS statement and see how they respond. They might say they are happy to hear from you, but they can't think of anyone at the moment. That's fine. You have got them thinking about you and pushed yourself to their top of mind list.

Be brave and make the calls to those former clients. We have found that people want to make referrals. It builds their status when they can say, "I got a guy/gal who can help you."

Professional Connections

No matter your business, you have a pipeline connected to other business people. For example, a realtor's network includes real estate attorneys, home inspectors, repair experts, cleaning companies, painters, and landscapers. Likewise, a copywriter's network connects with web designers, ad agencies, photographers, news outlets, book publishers, and editors.

These two professions have independent networks of connections. Still, they are likely to intersect when the Realtor needs a photographer or copy written and when the writer wants her office painted and the gutters fixed.

"Who do you know?" is a great question to send through your business pipeline. The writer can ask the photographer, "Who do you know that needs a video script?" The Realtor can check with the painter to see who is sprucing up their home to get it ready for sale. The only dumb question is the one not asked.

Circle of Influence

Even the most introverted person has a core of about 200 people in their Circle of Influence. These are people they *know, like, and trust*; and feel the same way about them. Of those 200 people, each of them has another 200 connections.

For instance, Pat and Martin each have 200 connections that don't overlap. Pat doesn't need to be a perfect referral for all of Martin's 200 connections, but he is probably a match for five or ten. This is more than enough because each of those folks has their own connections.

Referrals are like tossing a pebble into a pond and watching the ripples expand endlessly. Your RSM positioning statement is your pebble; don't be afraid to use it.

Making It Work

An insurance agent Martin used took several years to win over a top nationally known realtor. He did it by showing up regularly with the best apples or some other luscious thing, dropping them off, and saying, "Hi. I just want to drop these off. My long-term goal is to be your number one referral for insurance."

The Realtor responded, "We already have one." He said, "I know." And then he came back. And then he came back. And then he came back. And then he came back. And now he's featured on her private moving truck going around Raleigh.

Referrals are not the short game. You must be willing to consistently invest in networking so that people know, like, trust, and remember you as their go-to for the products and services you offer and as the person who knows all the best people.

Go Deep

When you work with corporate entities and agencies, you should expect that your key contacts will change. They may get promoted, move to another company, or even start their own. All the goodwill you have built with that key person travels with them.

On the upside, they may invite you to work with them in a new capacity. On the downside, if they are your only contact with that entity, you have just lost a great client.

You can avoid losing out by going deeper into your connections to the organization. For example, identify and connect with Number Two, the gatekeeper, and your key contact's boss.

The second in charge and the gatekeeper are pretty easy to identify, and you always want to show them respect and acknowledge that they are also a cornerstone of your success. While the lower-level connections are not the decision-makers on your projects, they are influencers.

This doesn't mean you have to bring flowers and candy or tickets to the local event every time you show up. It means that you should know them by name and be interested in them, and goodies now and then won't hurt.

You can connect with their boss by sending a handwritten thank you note to acknowledge the business, rave about their team's excellence, and assure them they can contact you with any questions. You can also refer people to their business.

By going deep, you are building your reputation as an attentive, thoughtful business person who wants to see all the boats in your network rise on the high tide.

Get Connected

Networking doesn't happen monthly at the Chamber of Commerce meeting or at formal networking sessions. Instead, networking happens when you run into someone at the coffee shop, when you use social media, when you attend a seminar or workshop, and when you ask, "Who do you know...?" to find the right someone with the best solution.

We encourage you to build your connections list within the next 30 days with clients, colleagues, and complementary businesses. It starts with what used to be a Rolodex but now it is more likely your email list. Add on to that your connections on social media like LinkedIn, Facebook (business, not personal, please), Alignable, Instagram, and whatever new platform pops up to usurp these.

Every social media platform has ground rules that we follow to make our businesses approachable and captivating. We consciously adjust our message depending on our platform and who we are talking to. Be sure that you are using language that resonates with your target audience.

Build your connections by adding value to the online conversations. For example, offer a tip for doing business better, a suggestion for a great tool or resource, or give a shout-out to a connection for their recent award or promotion. Use your social media to demonstrate that you are a valuable business partner willing to offer a solution or find someone with the right solution.

Get to be the go-to person for referrals by staying active with positive, helpful information in your posts. If you can't say something nice, you're not trying hard enough.

Reward Referrals

The absolute best way to reward a referral is with another referral. Someone sends you a new client, and then you send someone who needs the solution they offer. As a result, you will each build bigger and broader networks.

Martin wanted to get a Christmas present for his home support team. Knowing that they like eco-friendly products and were knowledgeable about wellness, he went to his favorite local health food store. He told the store owner, "I want to get two gift certificates for the people that take care of me, and I want it so that they know about you because I'd like them to start doing business with you."

"The owner not only got them out, but she also made a special deal that was a win-win for them and me. They were excited when they got the gift certificates and went to the store. I created the relationship. And now they're regular clients at the store," says Martin. "Who's top-of-mind for future things? I am. To stay top-of-mind, pay back with a referral, connect two, and think local."

Half your job is giving referrals; maybe more than half. The idea is that you are making connections between the people that you know, like, and trust. Their connection wouldn't happen without you, and they want to return the favor.

You can keep your network visible while keeping yourself top-of-mind by posting a picture on social media. When you stop at your local diner and see a referral partner, snap a smiling photo and give it a happy caption. "Landscaper Wendy grabbed coffee at the Starlight Diner this morning and told me the best way to get rid of fire ants." You establish their humanity and expertise and give them a shout-out with one quick click.

You may have noticed that we're not talking about finder's fees or a percentage of the sale in return for the referral. That's because this RMS works best when you are not focused on the dollars but the value of the referral. Follow the process by inviting participation, and everyone comes out ahead.

Your mindset needs to be that you have something of great value and are a consistent and responsive referral partner. You can start doing this today. Get going!

CHAPTER 4

ENERGIZE YOUR RELATIONSHIP MARKETING

"Loyal customers, they do not just come back, they do not
simply recommend you, they insist that their friends do
business with you."
Chip R. Bell, Founder at the Chip Bell Group

We've given you the basics of building your RMS machine: clarifying who
you serve and how, identifying and coaching your referral partners, and
asking every client for referrals. With that foundation, you're ready to
look at different ways to make those valuable referral connections.

The Guided Meeting

Think of when you are meeting with a client, and it dawns on you that they need additional solutions that you can't provide. For instance, Jane is a copywriter meeting with a client to update their website copy. As Jane reviews the site, she can see that it is outdated and doesn't function very well. The client knows it, too, but they don't have a connection for website development.

Jane shows the client samples of websites she has worked on with a web designer, Telly, and discusses how Telly could improve the old site. Then Jane says, "Let me set up a meeting with you and Telly so you can get more details." The client is relieved to connect to a trusted web designer and appreciates that Jane was thinking beyond her role as a writer to make them look great.

Send a Referral Email

When you want to connect with two or three people, email is one of the easiest ways. In your message, you will address the value and need of each person, share their contact email, and ask them to follow up with you ASAP, so you know they have connected. Here's a simplified plan:

The Referral Email

What do they need, and who do you know can supply it?

- Be sure you understand the need and timeline.

- Confirm with the referral that they are willing and able to meet the expectations

- Only recommend people who you *know*, *like*, and *trust*.

Be clear that you are only making an introduction. No guarantees!

- Your task is to introduce the people and provide initial contact information.

- You should be able to provide a robust description of their talents.

- The subject line should include the word "Introduction" so that it is easy to find.

Break your messages out to each person.

- Remind each party why they are being connected.

- Remind each party how they are expected to serve.

- Give additional instructions for follow-up with you, positive or negative.

This sounds like a lot of stuff, but it is just a short message. After that, it is up to them to do the work!

Here is an example.

```
From: Martin Brossman

To: Larry, Jane, and Whitney

RE: Introductions to Key Resources

I am happy to introduce you to each other as I can see
great value in your work.
```

Larry: Jane is a copywriter who listens closely to her clients to create a precisely targeted message in their voice and words. I talked to her on the phone, and she says she can assist with reaching potential customers and maintaining compliance for your client. Also, please schedule a meeting with Whitney soon. He knows about your excellent work.

Jane: Larry does web design work, develops small business marketing programs, and is a great guy. He is helping the CBD/Hemp farmer we spoke about.

Whitney: You should be aware of both Larry and Jane as you may find them helpful for reaching out to new clients.

Please reach out to each other ASAP and let me know if this is a positive partnership.

Martin
(contact information)

Planting the Seed

Think of yourself as a gardener. This is where you just let the referral/client know a specific referral partner will contact them and that the connection will be beneficial.

For instance, Pat says, "Hey, listen, you were talking about something the other day, and you said you needed somebody who knew the XYZ Protocol. I know somebody. It's Martin Brossman. I'm going to ask him to reach out to you. What's the best way for him to contact you?"

When you are paying attention to your client, you are listening for ways to be of service to them. One of those ways is connecting them with people with other skills, knowledge, and connections that will be helpful to them.

You become a valuable partner in their success. Not just because you heard that they had a need, but that you are willing to connect them to your broader network, it's a win for everyone.

Your job is to offer the connection, ensure that the client is receptive, and then make the connection. By planting this seed, you are growing their network and yours.

Sharing Door-to-Door and Desk-to-Desk

Sharing what you know is a great way to connect without making a pitch. It shows that you are informed, knowledgeable, and willing to assist. Just be sure you're giving out good solid information that is useful to your connections and potential clients. There are two great ways to share - the Old School process of actually knocking on doors and the New School which utilizes social media.

Old School

When there is construction work in your neighborhood, getting a door hanger or a postcard that tells you the Jones family is getting a new solar system from Acme Solar is not unusual. The company may even send a representative to your door to introduce themselves, apologize for the temporary disruption, and give a little insight into what the Jones' are doing, in case you want to keep up with them.

This is great information that your contact will gladly share with their neighbors as they scrutinize the job, the cost, and the competency of your team. That personal touch of letting the neighbors know what's going on elevates your company in their view. You are top-of-mind because you showed that you cared enough about their inconvenience to keep them informed. You've certainly made yourself stand out from the competition.

New School

You can also use social media to do the same thing. Whether you are building websites or fences, a great picture and an exciting caption will make people think they could also use an upgrade. But, again, include specifics about the product or service to make the announcement more enticing.

Everyone who graduates from Martin's Social Media Marketing Program gets their picture taken with Martin announcing they have just earned their certificate. This little bit of sharing builds interest for Martin's program and the graduate who is now ready to make a difference for your business.

When you post these pictures or hand out a flier, ensure you have a link to your website so people can further explore your options, process, and make that important connection.

Referral Pricing

If you still find it challenging to ask for referrals, here's a way to couch that lets the client decide. When it comes to the pricing questions, you can answer, "Would you like the referral price or the standard price?" The inquisitive prospect will ask about the difference. You respond with, "If you refer three people to us within 90 days, you'll get a 10% discount. I prefer to give you those savings rather than spend that money on advertising, and if you agree to send me three referrals, I can apply that discount now."

Referral Discount

When a client provides you with a referral, you can thank them with a discount on their next purchase. It lets them know that you appreciate and recognize their referral. It also puts you back top-of-mind with them and may lead to other referrals.

Case Study

Working for referrals is an option for people who are just getting started in business. You could be building websites, landscaping, or providing personal services like wellness or aesthetics. Be very selective and identify clients who are keystones of your marketplace. The website designer could select a non-profit organization. The landscaper would find a visible home that needs curb appeal. The personal services would identify community leaders who will become walking talking billboards for their new business.

Explain to them that you are just starting your business and offer your credentials. Tell them they are case studies for your portfolio, and in exchange, you would appreciate three referrals to others who could use your products or services. Avoid the word "FREE" because 1. It is not free, and 2. The cost is the commitment of three referrals.

In each situation, use the same process as if you were getting paid cash rather than referrals. You will assess their needs, identify the solution, and provide the services as if they were exchanging dollars rather than referrals for your services. Frankly, these referrals will be worth much more than the cost of your initial case study. They will be the springboard for your business.

Hold a Contest

Most people love to play, and those who don't won't. Holding a contest is a great way to get your current clients and referral partners to light up your business. You can hand out a coupon (or email it) and tell your customers to share it with someone who could use your products or services. Tell them they are entered into a drawing for a prize when the coupon is redeemed. The prize can be a gift basket of products, a discounted or free service, or an award from another referral partner like a local restaurant or spa.

If you have a small retail business, keep a fishbowl for the coupons and use a tally sheet. For larger corporate projects, look into software like Upviral.com to manage your contest. Finally, remember to acknowledge the winner on all your social media. Again, this makes people aware that you offer tremendous value to your customers and clients.

Non-Profit Referrals

Pick an organization that is close to your heart and is compatible with your business. For instance, you're a building contractor, and when you have leftover materials, you donate them to Habitat for Humanity or their Restore outlet. After a while, they start to recognize that you are a constant presence and may soon ask you for assistance on a build. Or one of their board members may think of you for their next remodeling job at their residence.

Keep in mind that just like every other referral technique, giving is the way to start, and you never know where it may pay off.

Gamify Referrals

In some industries, you can offer to pay a customer for multiple referrals and effectively give them their product at no cost – except for the referrals. Of course, not everyone will take you up on it, but if you offer, "When you send five people to me, I'm going to give you back 20% of your cost for each person you send to me that makes a purchase. So if you send five people, you'll get a 100% rebate. If you send two people, I will honor my offer and provide you with a 40% rebate."

Explain that you provide the rebate to keep your marketing costs down and allow you to spend more time focused on your clients. You will almost see the wheels turning as your customer sorts through the people they know who would benefit from connecting with you and figuring out where they will spend that rebate money.

Meet Up at Events

There may be someone you've wanted to talk to, but you just haven't connected yet. You may learn on social media that they are planning to attend the same Chamber Event, community program, or training session that you have on your calendar; reach out to them. Send them a direct message, an email, or a text, and let them know you'd appreciate making a face-to-face connection.

Pat keeps an index card in his pocket with the people he wants to meet at an event. It helps remind him who he is looking for and reminds him of anyone who ends up being a no-show. Back at his desk, he can now send notes to the people he met and genuinely inquire about the no-show folks.

Remember

Networking events (any activity that involves cohorts, colleagues, and competitors); you are not there to sell anything. The event is to meet with people to share your values. You are there to learn about other people: their business, needs, and goals. And then (if you get a positive feeling), set up a follow-up for a quick coffee to delve deeper and see how your network might help them. You will receive more referrals if you give more referrals.

Say Thanks!

At the end of your first mini-meeting, sure you can say, "Thanks for your time! It was great to meet you!" Then, of course, you could zip out a text, leave a voice message, or send an email. But if you want to make a strong impression, send a handwritten note. It can be as simple as a postcard or as impressive as a monogrammed notecard.

Here's a sample: *"Hey, Martin, it was great meeting you at the Chamber event. I look forward to seeing you in the future."* Writing the note and addressing the envelope takes minutes, but the effect is long-lasting. (By the way, use black ink and hand-address the envelope, too.)

Some people carry postcards or note cards in their cars so that as soon as they leave an event, they can begin writing their thank you notes and even drop them in the mail that day or evening. Otherwise, keep them in your desk with postage stamps, so you have no excuse for not making a great impression.

Write Recommendations

A social media recommendation is another example of building your credentials while boosting someone else. By writing a sincere recommendation for another business person, you are expanding their reach through your social media network, boosting their self-esteem, and showing appreciation for their work. It also puts you top of mind with them and their network as people will comment on your encouraging words.

Pay It Forward

You should have noticed a common thread in all these techniques for building your business through relationship marketing. Give first, and it will come back to you. Give your full attention to the people you meet and ask open-ended questions to learn about their business and goals. Next, give your clients access to your network by referring them to those who can provide solutions that you can't. Finally, offer value to the referrals by ensuring they are a match and fulfill their task. You will be amazed at how this will come back to you.

CHAPTER 5

MARKETING PARTNERSHIPS

"People influence people. Nothing influences people more
than a recommendation from a trusted friend. A trusted
referral influences people more than the best broadcast
message. A trusted referral is the Holy Grail of advertising."
Mark Zuckerberg, Facebook

Now that you know how to give referrals and follow up on them, we need
to step back just a tiny bit. Yes, the people that you refer to are people
you know, like, and trust. That's the baseline. The truth is, you should
think of yourself as a true partner who understands their business and
their ideal client, as well as you know your own. This knowledge ensures
that the referrals you provide are appropriate for your partner, and you
should anticipate that they will reciprocate similarly.

Get Prepared

When you connect with a referral partner, take the time to talk with them about their business, how they market, and who they market to.

For instance, an interior designer has referral partners for wallpaper, painting, plumbing, electrical, and flooring. Her flooring partners are particular about their preferred customers. One does wood floor installation, another refinishing, a third does ceramic tile and vinyl plank, and the fourth only does custom decorative tile in small areas.

The designer must know which flooring partner will be the right one to work with her client. If her client is budget-conscious, she'll recommend a partner that works with ceramic and vinyl planks. On the other hand, a big-budget client who wants cherry flooring and a stunning entry would be a match for the wood installer and the custom tile setter.

Knowing your referral partners well means that you will look brilliant when you recommend them because you can articulate what they do and who they work with.

Shared Social Media Marketing

You and your referral partners can easily set up shared marketing programs to enhance and reinforce your connection. Social media is the fastest way to let the world know who is in your network. When you meet with your partners, snap a picture (even if it is a virtual meeting), and you can post it on your networks with a caption telling how you are working together.

Martin does this regularly when he grabs coffee or lunch with a colleague. You'll see their smiling faces, and he'll add a caption that reads, "Met with

Roxanne today in Fuquay-Varina to talk about marketing her adaptive clothing business." He'll also supply links to Roxanne's website or social media business profile. And she'll do the same for Martin, except her caption would read, "Met with Martin today in Fuquay-Varina to learn the best practices for relationship marketing. "

Each partner has independent connections, some will overlap, but everyone will know that Martin thinks highly of Roxanne and vice versa. They have just endorsed and marketed each other to their respective networks.

Whoever sees the post will now have them top of mind; Martin for relationship marketing and Roxanne for adaptive clothing.

Shared Direct Marketing

Imagine your referral partner has added a product or service that could benefit your connections, and you want to inform them quickly and efficiently. First, use the direct marketing approach. Old school direct marketing meant sending a hardcopy letter. Today you'll more likely send an email to a selected segment of your mailing list to endorse one of your referral partners.

For example, Martin has a course coming up on identifying your target market. Pat found out about it through social media and will certainly share the information, but he wants to go further and get the message out directly to people in his network that could most benefit. He creates an endorsement for Martin's class and cites the benefits of attending.

```
Dear Jane,

I just want to let you know that my colleague Martin
Brossman will be offering an online 90-minute seminar:
```

Your Target Market Customer Persona - Clarify and Identify Your Buyer.

Martin is dedicated to helping small business owners succeed in their markets by increasing their visibility and pinpointing their ideal clients.

In this class, Martin will show you how to create your Ideal Customer Persona customer persona, find the best media to reach them, and what you need to tell them so that they will commit to you.

Use this link to sign up for the class next Tuesday at 7:30 PM, and let me know how it goes!

All the best,

Pat

Will everyone that Pat invites sign up for the class? Not necessarily, but his contacts are grateful that he thought enough of them to share this opportunity. It also allows the recipient to forward it to someone in their network, saying, "Pat always shares good stuff. This seminar might be of interest to you. I am planning to attend."

You can also use this Direct Marketing technique when you want to recognize your insurance agent, attorney, shoemaker, or baker for providing you with an outstanding experience. Of course, it takes a little more effort than a quick social media post, but you can see how the ripple effect can benefit so many people.

Marketing Content

You may have noticed in both the Social Media post and the Direct Marketing piece that price was never mentioned. Price is not how people decide to buy or not. Value is the deciding factor. Buyers need to know what value your product or service brings to their life. Therefore, all your marketing materials need to educate the consumer so that they want to learn more about you to ensure your referral partners and your potential customers understand your value.

Postcards, flyers, social media posts, posters, blogs, pens, whatever you put out there for marketing should be educational. Marketing keeps you top of mind and gets your phone to ring, fills your inbox, or sends people to your website so that they can learn what you offer.

With relationship marketing, when Martin sends along the link to Jane's blog on *Conquering Stage Fright* to one or several of his clients, it is an endorsement of her services. Martin's only goal is to share that information to benefit his client. He does not need to start getting into her fees and services; the recipient can do that on their own. Instead, Martin's mission is to educate, connect, and spark interest in his connections. What usually happens is that the endorsement comes back many times over, so be thoughtful, generous, and educational.

Giving Testimonials

Earlier, we talked about testimonials. The testimonials that you give are more beneficial than the ones you get. That sounds counterintuitive, but let's look at how it works.

When you provide a sincere and knowledgeable testimonial for one of your networking partners, you raise their stock and yours. In addition, their image improves by your specific and glowing endorsement of their products, services, and skills. (Remember, it needs to be more than a few words. Make it at least a full sentence or two.)

Your reputation improves because you have stuck your neck out to endorse this person, and for the people who know, like, and trust you, that is a huge deal. You were intentional in your recommendation. You took the time and effort to point out their value, and in doing so, you have also demonstrated your expertise and the range of your network.

If Martin finds a coffeehouse he likes in East Podunk and provides a testimonial, people in his circle will drop in the next time they are up that way. They may even say, "Martin sent me!" so the owner knows how these people from afar have found his little café.

You create a buzz of information with your testimonials and are a great marketing partner.

Getting Testimonials

Of course, you still want to get testimonials for your clients. But, some of you may still be afraid to ask for it. Be fearless. Ask your clients and customers why they chose you. You may be surprised at their answer, as Pat was years ago when he was doing computer repair.

Pat faced a tough competitor, so he priced his repair service below their rate to capture more business. He got the business, but his accountant told him he was not earning enough to be viable. The accountant said he had to up his rate or close his doors.

Faced with that tough decision, Pat took the risk and asked his customers why they chose him for their computer repairs. The answer came back that it was the excellent service and turnaround time his company offered. With that knowledge, Pat raised his rates above his competitor's and continued to grow his business.

By getting those testimonials, Pat learned that it wasn't the price that brought his customers in; it was the value of being assured their computer would be repaired in under 24 hours.

Ask your clients why they chose you, and then share their answers on your website, at your store, through your social media, and in all your marketing. Also, request that they share it with other people in their network, so their connections will also see the value of doing business with you.

Business 101: Reciprocity

Again, if you are just starting, you should figure out how many referrals you can give out this week. Or, if you have been in business for a while, when you find you have an empty calendar, fill it up by making connections and getting out your referrals.

Start with the mindset of how you can help people do business better. Pay attention when people say they need something, whether it is an excellent mechanic, a commercial photographer, or a chiropractor. Then tap into your mental Rolodex* and make a connection.

Suddenly, you will see your calendar filling up with people who want to know more about you and how you can solve their personal and professional challenges. You will be their number one pain reliever not just because of what you do but also because of who you know.

That's the *"law of reciprocity"* kicking in, the desire for good people to do good things for good people. And that is how you become a great marketing partner for your connections.

*A once-popular system of organizing contacts and their business cards by holding them in a physical state as an alphabetized rotating file. - MB

CHAPTER 6

MARKETING POSITION: WHO DO YOU SERVE?

"If you do build a great experience, customers tell each other about that. Word of mouth is very powerful."
Jeff Bezos, Amazon

We have touched on identifying your ideal target market; now, we will dig deep to show you how to strategically position yourself in your marketplace. First, you will understand that narrowcasting is where the money is, while broadcasting is how to starve to death.

When you first start in business, part of you wants to believe that what you provide is for everyone, and it is not. But instead, you learn that you are the expert for a finite number of people who need, want, and are willing to pay for your products and services.

By being strategic, you narrowcast to the ideal people who are ready and willing to commit. You take control of your marketing, so it is laser-focused on those people rather than broadcast to those with no interest. Great marketing attracts those who should do business with you and repels all others.

Positioning separates you from your competitors. It instantly establishes what your clients should expect from you on quality, price, and service. For example, imagine traveling to Paris, France. You could stay at the Hotel Ritz or an Airbnb. Both places will provide you with a place to sleep, but each has a specific position in the marketplace.

Attract and Repel

Speaking of bed and breakfasts, one of Martin's favorites is Big Mill Bed & Breakfast in Williamston, North Carolina. Chloe Tuttle is the innkeeper and a professional chef. However, she doesn't like making breakfast, so instead, she offers her guests granola, jam and bread, fresh milk, orange juice, and the fixings for coffee. Anyone on the staff can easily set up the breakfast, and it's in the room ready when the guests arrive.

When potential guests call and start asking about the expected lavish breakfast, Chloe resets their expectations and, if necessary, redirects them to another B&B that will better match their ideal. Since she has narrowcasted her market, she is usually fully booked. Recently, Chloe added kitchenettes to each unit and has converted to primarily long-term stays for professionals and adventurous vacationers.

Chloe has attended many of Martin's marketing classes, and he frequently uses her business as an example of snagging a well-defined position in a cluttered market. Occasionally, a student will wonder why she didn't just offer a bigger breakfast and capture the rest of the market.

First of all, she didn't want to. Secondly, by defining her Big Mill as the place to go and relax without a schedule or intrusion, she attracts that customer who is thrilled to be there. They don't have to get up in the morning and be friendly with strangers; they can eat when they like and still have the B&B atmosphere of a cozy room on a working farm.

If you are stuck trying to identify your ideal customer, think about the people you don't want to serve. Then, think of the people that take up 80% of your time and give you 20% of your profit.

Another of Martin's marketing students has a bakery specializing in dairy-free, gluten-free, and nut-free pastries and cakes for people with allergies. She volunteered that one of her least favorite customers asked where the bakery gets its eggs and other ingredients. At first, the baker thought she should make a list identifying the sources for all her makings and have that at the ready for customers like the egg lady.

Martin said, "Please don't make that list. Do you think the egg lady and others like her will be satisfied with that list?" The baker paused for a minute, then replied, "No." She realized that by doing that, she would encourage picky customers she could never satisfy.

Instead of making that list, the baker could use her time to create a flyer that promotes their allergy-free products and slips it in with every purchase. That little bit of educational marketing will mean a lot to her committed customers, who already trust her skills and ingredients. It reminds them to come back for more goodies and to tell others about the allergy-free options.

As a business owner, it is up to you to purposefully attract the right customers and repel (redirect) the people who are not your ideal.

Competition: Conquer or Cooperate

Years ago, Pat lived in Fraser, Colorado, a small rural town near the Winter Park ski area. He had established a successful computer tech shop and was very involved in the community. Then, a new guy, formerly at Microsoft, came to town, introduced himself, and announced that he planned to put Pat out of business.

At first, Pat thought he was just posturing and instead offered that the two businesses could co-exist because there were plenty of customers within the region and many things his shop didn't offer that were needed. The new competitor explained that he wanted the whole market and didn't need to cooperate, "it was just business".

The competitor started advertising. So, Pat did as well, but his ads offered computer parts at wholesale prices. Concentrating on his advantage of a tech team providing services that his competitor did not have.

While we truly believe in value over price, this was a tactical move, and it worked. The competitor was livid and phoned Pat to complain about his below market pricing.

Pat explained that if he were going to be put out of business he was going to make it very hard and expensive for his competition. He knew he had supportive clients who would stick with him, so he looked at this challenge as an opportunity to gain more market share with this pricing.

The competitor had energized the market, and good business people like competition. He also knew it was only a matter of time before the business climate changed this competitor's "take over" strategy.

Shortly afterward, as Pat's business grew and he expanded into new products and services the region needed, he ended up purchasing the competing business and grew to become the Internet Service Provider with over 3000 rural customers.

Competition is good and you should actively look for it locally or outside your service area. But, it's best to cooperate; we call it "coopetition".

Create Your Ideal Customer Persona

Your customer persona is a visual manifestation of your ideal client. You create the customer persona by reviewing the attributes of your best customers. For example, you want to know where they live and work, their age, their interests, the type of car they drive, where they shop, family status, and personal attitude.

The shopper who heads to the health food store for organic almond milk is not the same consumer who regularly drops into the convenience store for a jug of milk. Just from reading this, you visualized two very different people even if their demographic information (age, income, family size, homeowner, and location) matches.

Once you have taken the time to identify your ideal customer persona, you can effectively and efficiently target your marketing to bring them into your business. The customer persona sharpens your laser focus on your position in your marketplace.

Your customer persona is the quickest and cleanest way to communicate the clients you serve to your referral partners. The clear visual means your marketing partners know exactly who to send your way.

Getting What You Want

As you first start out in business, your ideal client may not materialize as you planned.

Essentially, we are encouraging you to start backward. Imagine your perfect business. Visualize the systems and processes you have in place, the products and services you offer, and that ideal client you want to serve. Then ask yourself two questions:

1. "Does this market exist?" If you can't find something your market cares about, you don't have a market. That may be why somebody's business isn't reaching the levels it could or should be.

2. "What makes me different?" If you are unsure, ask your current customers or clients what makes them come to you.

For instance, Pat knew a young man, Billy, who was an exceptional financial planner. He had an excellent education and has been passionate about investing since he was a teenager. His clients genuinely appreciated his service and expertise. He envisioned his market as high-net-worth investors actively interested in their portfolios.

His market did exist, but those people thought of him as a kid and felt more comfortable with a more mature person. Pat suggested to Billy that he offer guidance to people who were carrying student debt.

By taking that position in the market, Billy became a trusted expert for the offspring of those high-net-worth parents. As the parents became aware of Billy's expertise, they started turning to him for financial solutions.

Once you start getting traction on your position with your current clients, you can create a marketing message that supports this position.

Positioned, Not Pigeonholed

Carving out your niche market does not restrict you to that one category. The cool thing about a position is that other opportunities will show up once you claim it. For example, Pat approached a bookkeeper who primarily worked with restaurants and suggested targeting people in Multi-Level Marketing (MLM). His timely suggestion helped her transition from restaurants where the competition was stiff to MLM owners who became her instant referral network.

A well-defined position helps you stand out from your crowded field. The market does not need another person who does what you do; it needs the *difference* you bring *with what you do*.

Make a list of all the benefits your business offers the market. After creating this list, keep only those *truly unique* entries. These benefits could be as tangible as a superb location with easy access or as intangible as your problem-solving skills.

To confirm your list of unique benefits, go back to the people who have hired you and ask them point-blank why they chose you. Then, follow up with questions about what you could do to serve them better, and then use this information to zero in on your target market.

Colleen is an excellent social media marketer. She could work for just about anyone, but she recognized that tradespeople don't have the time or energy to do social media. As a result, she has captured an underserved market by working with plumbers, carpenters, and electricians.

Once you recognize what makes you unique (your knowledge, service, products, and solutions), you will be able to direct your marketing to the people who need you most.

Marketing is Education

Once you identify your target, your marketing program educates your potential clients. For instance, Pat had been encouraged to see a chiropractor for his sore back, but he thought they were on the fringe of health care. However, after he learned about their training and techniques and experienced relief without drugs, he became a huge proponent of chiropractic practices, goes regularly, and is a great referrer.

Price is not a factor in marketing. However, value is vital because anyone can compete with you on price. Your value is unique, not your pricing; so remember to keep pricing out of your marketing.

Think of it this way, CarMax does not sell the least expensive cars; they sell vehicles with the least amount of haggling. That unique offering sets them apart from every other used car lot.

You must consider your potential client's needs and how they will search for that information. For example, if you want the best price when looking for car insurance, you'll likely enter "cheap car insurance" into your internet search engine. Since cheap equates to inferior, an insurance agency would avoid using that word in their marketing unless it was part of a blog explaining why cheap car insurance can be expensive. So again, it is an opportunity to educate your potential client using terms that resonate.

A scuba instructor got a one-star review for not clearly explaining the importance of the medical form for new students. The instructor understood that students needed a doctor's signature on the form before entering the water. Still, his students weren't clear about the instructions and were disappointed when the missing signature prohibited them from participating in the class.

In response to negative feedback, the scuba instructor created a video for his website that clearly explained how to fill out the medical form and the requirement for the doctor's sign-off before starting the class. While his educational video provided instruction for potential students, it also gave them a chance to meet him virtually and make a connection. In addition, he positioned himself as a careful, caring instructor.

Your goal is to create a marketing plan that turns your prospects into raving fans. Your marketing program will educate and entice them to come to you for a solution. Then, when you provide the products or services they need in a positively unforgettable manner, you will have a new referral marketer on your team: a thrilled customer.

Staking a position in your marketplace allows you to identify who you work with and how you provide products and services to your target. You do not want to be for everyone. You want to be the best option for your ideal client.

Next, we will work on defining your Unique Value Proposition. Again, *how* you answer the question, "What do you do?" will get people interested in you and your solutions.

CHAPTER 7

UNIQUE VALUE PROPOSITION/YOUR MESSAGE

"Word-of-mouth marketing isn't about giving customers talking points as if they were brand spokespeople. It's about delivering an exceptional customer experience that makes customers want to recommend you."

Deborah Eastman, CMO, Satmetrix

Okay, you have profiled your ideal customer, established your market position, and now you need to create the message that quickly, succinctly, and memorably states the value of doing business with you. That message is called a Unique Value Proposition (UVP), and it is not an elevator speech or a pitch of any type. Instead, it is a quick answer to "What do you do?" that leaves people intrigued enough to ask more questions.

Why Should You Use the UVP?

Your first meeting is when you get to know people. You find out what you have in common and if and how you might extend the relationship. Like dating, you don't start the evening with a proposal (or a proposition) that would scare people away from you.

You know what it feels like to have someone stuffing their business card in your hand with the expectation that you are their next sale. That is not relationship marketing.

By consistently using your UVP, you have a perfect, powerful answer to "What do you do?" And yet, it is not a pitch. It is a declaration of your abilities and who you work best with. Your UVP is a tool to get into people's circles of influence. You are working to get referred. You are working to get people into the relationship marketing structure and your word-of-mouth system. That is a system that will enable you to do good business continuously.

They are going to ask you what you do for a living, and you are going to tell them what you do for people that actually need your product or service and who you are meant to serve. So, you will start building your relationship with this potential colleague by sharing your values and learning about theirs.

Values Reviewed

Your *values* are the reason people like working with you. They are the benefits you provide for your specific market. Therefore, you must have values that resonate with them and that serve your clients so they will return to you and refer other people (who are like them) to you.

Think about big retailers like Walmart and Target. At first glance, some people may assume these retailers serve the same customers, but they don't. For example, Walmart spent years talking about how they were the cheapest place to shop. Then Target popped on the scene and clarified that their stores, products, and services were better and that their prices were very competitive. Think about it; you don't see Target shopper memes on social media. If you are shopping price, you go to Walmart; that is their brand. If you want better quality, you go to Target because that is their brand.

Will you find Walmart shoppers at Target? Probably. Will you find Target shoppers at Walmart, also probably, but shoppers for each brand have an allegiance to one and will spend most of their dollars at the one that matches their values. So, what do they want, the cheaper price or the better product?

A word of caution, price is not the best "value" to lead with for your Unique Value Proposition. For example, saying you have the least expensive auto body shop in town will sound fishy. It may be true that your hourly rate is the lowest in the area, but what people want to know is how quickly you can take their vehicle from homely to handsome. In addition, people want to know that your auto body team looks for the hidden damage after an accident, so that their vehicle is not just good-looking but also road worthy.

The benefits of working with you (your value) are your personality, protocols, and performance. Think of what you do and how you do it that makes you stand out and above the others in your field.

What do they love?

Self-reflection can be difficult, so if you are unsure what your clients love about you, just ask them. You will notice that many medical offices are sending out digital and snail mail questionnaires to find out what you thought about your last visit. They ask about wait times, services provided, and how the staff made you feel during your appointment.

You can ask similar questions. The easiest way is to sincerely approach your client and say, "What did you like/love about working with me (us)? What did we do that made you feel great? Why would you work with us again?"

You can also ask your referral partners and the people in your referral group other questions to get a different viewpoint on what people value from your industry. Since they know your industry, ask them: "What are people not doing in my industry that you would love them to do for you? What could people in my industry do that would thrill you? What can we do that would have the most impact on supporting you or your business?" When you ask those questions, let your colleagues know that they don't have to answer at that moment. Give them a chance to think about it and share it with you in the next week or so.

Remember to follow up with them, too! The follow-up makes it clear that your request is sincere and that you put great stock in their opinion. Also, that follow-up contact is your chance to return the favor and say, "Here's what I think would be an impressive value for someone in your industry!"

Following up on these questions for your clients and colleagues has the additional value of creating another opportunity to connect with them, reminding them of the value you provided them, and getting back to top of mind with them.

The Formula

Once you truly understand the value you bring to your clients, you are ready to build your UVP. Part 1 is your action and the benefit you provide, and Part 2 is how you do the things you do.

For example, let's look at Martin's UVP: "I teach small businesses how to make more money without spending more money." It has all the elements: his target market, action, and benefits.

Part 1

For your initial response, start with an *action* word, such as: teach, guide, relieve, direct, transform, prevent, create, or show. Include your target market, and close with the *benefit you provide*.

Accountant: I ensure | *small retailers* | *stay off the IRS radar*.

Stylist: I transform *women* into *confident, natural beauties*.

Chiropractor: I give *contractors* more *pain-free work days*.

Martin: I teach *small businesses* how to *make more money without spending more money*.

These short answers beg the question, "Tell me more! How do you do this?" So get your answer ready.

Part 2

When asked, "Tell me more..." you present your *how* by describing your techniques, tools, or protocols to deliver the best possible service and outcome.

Accountant: By maintaining monthly communication and insisting on quarterly reviews.

```
Stylist: I listen closely to my client's desires and use
eco-friendly products.

Chiropractor: My dad was a carpenter; I'm committed to
preventing tradespeople from working in pain.

Martin: By teaching them to use relationship marketing
and word-of-mouth advertising to narrowcast into their
target market.
```

Creating this core message quickly and clearly demonstrates the benefits of doing business with *you*. Of course, other people provide what you do, but the benefits of how *you* serve your particular clientele make you stand out from those others.

Having your Unique Value Proposition at the ready makes it so much easier for people to either connect with you or make connections for you.

In the above example, the chiropractor seeks contractors (their target market) to provide pain-free work days. He may be speaking to a realtor who doesn't need his services, but she may know contractors who could benefit from knowing about this particular chiropractor. That's how networking works!

You worked so hard to identify your client customer persona; now, your UVP speaks directly to them and those who know them. Your UVP is the magic formula for your relationship marketing system.

As a reminder, you are not selling anything. Instead, you are educating potential networking partners about what is unique to your business.

Stuff Happens

Imagine you have the magic formula (UVP) and are fired up for your next networking event. You stroll in ready to greet someone and get the conversations rolling when an unknown person rushes up and says, "Hi! I'm *Really Annoying*, here's my card; I have what you need! Take my card... I know I can help you, save you money, make you money, make you taller/thinner/happier/smarter, whatever. AND! I am the best at it. See ya!" POOF! They are off to their next target.

And thankfully, they are gone. You take a deep breath, gather your wits, and turn to the stranger next to you and say, "Hi, tell me about your business!"

"Wait, what? They are supposed to ask me!" is what you're thinking. And you are right. They are. And they will, but you've got to figure that nothing will happen if nobody asks.

Two things are likely to happen now. One is they will also have a UVP, and you'll say, "Tell me more!" And they will. Then they will ask, "What do you do?" Since you practiced your UVP, the words will roll off your tongue, and they will also ask how *you* do what you do. You both win! Congrats.

What Do You Love?

You might find this an odd question, but when you get people to talk about their passion, you'll have a better idea of who they ideally serve and not just how they do it but why. So, when you want to learn more about a potential referral partner, ask them, "What do you love about what you do?" They will get thoughtful, animated, and excited to have the opportunity to answer that question. You will be the best conversationalist because you let them expound about their passion, and you listen. People love talking about what they do and rarely get a chance to do so. Let them, and they will remember you.

When asked what he loves about teaching small businesses to succeed, Martin responded: "What I love is when I get messages after a class from students who are so excited about their results; they wanted to let me know. Just recently, I got a text from a guy saying, 'Let me show you, I listened in class!' And his text included an image showing how he had applied something he learned. Yes! That's a real win. If I can get my students so excited, they want to come back and tell me, then it really makes my day!"

Combining your UVP with your phenomenal conversation skills (aka asking questions and then listening), you will build your referral network deep and wide.

Now get out there! In the next chapter, we will discuss how to be sure you are ready to do business.

CHAPTER 8

READY, FIRE, AIM!

"We take most of the money that we could have spent on paid marketing and instead put it back into the customer experience. Then we let the customer be our marketing. Historically, our number one growth driver has been from repeat customers and word-of-mouth."
Tony Hseih, Zappos CEO

When we started building this program on relationship marketing for our readers, we made an assumption. That assumption was that you are ready to do business. We assume that you have selected a product or service and have researched its value in your marketplace. And, from that research, you have decided that you have something that needs to come to market. That's great!

Notice that we didn't require that you have your logo, business cards, website, or marketing plan ready to go or up and running. Instead, we want you to know that you can start doing business without any of those things. So, if you've been using the lack of marketing collateral as an excuse to avoid pursuing your business goal, stop it!

Those ancillary things are not what is in your way. Your mindset is the big hurdle.

Throughout this training, we have coached you to understand who needs what you offer, how to identify and connect to those people, and most importantly, how to build a relationship marketing network that will create a river of business flowing directly to you.

Should you have a website, business cards, and all the other business trappings? Yeah, most likely, especially the business cards. But here's the thing, you can get out there now and start connecting to people and building your network even without all that other stuff. Go! Get started!

The Other Stuff

When it is time to create your logo, website, and marketing messages (or update it to match your new understanding of your target customer persona), ensure each element speaks to your market with the same consistent message. Then, with your branding all pulled together, be sure to use your logo and your company colors to create an instant correlation between you/your product and who you serve.

Use your Unique Value Proposition in print, online, and in person. It sums up who you are, who you serve, and how you differ from others in your industry. Using your UVP as the basis for your marketing message, you will always be on track to connect to the right people.

That Sums it Up

As Martin Brossman says, "Relationship marketing improves your business with more income, more enjoyable customers, and a more fulfilling life since you put yourself into a service mindset. You are serving your ideal customers and your networking partners. What could be better than that?"

We have provided you with a system with a few simple rules: Know your product, know your target market, know your value, and start connecting.

You are ready to become an excellent relationship marketing partner. Get started by joining a referral network, a BNI group, a small business round-table, your Chamber of Commerce, or any group of like-minded people you can get to know, like, and trust.

Identify the types of people that you're currently referring to. Take note of the people you're already working with and *enjoy* working with. Hang out with people whose work you already love to stay connected to compatible people. And again, as stated in the training, find people already serving in the same pipeline as you.

Remember the Realtor? She is serving current and potential home-owners. Her network includes the tradespeople who supply and maintain a home, from landscapers to plumbers and interior designers to pest removal. Who serves the same people that you do? Connect with them to make your network expand exponentially!

Your network is your referral toolbox. And those tools are jewel encrusted because you already know, like, and trust the people in your network. So when you make a referral from your network, you have confidence that your connection will provide at least the same level of product or service that you would provide. As you use your network, it will grow, as will your reputation for being the go-to person for solid referrals.

Be a Farmer

The difference between marketing and relationship marketing is the difference between hunting and farming. When hunting for business, you are trying to trap a customer. While you desperately want to get an elephant, all you might catch is chipmunks. So you won't starve, but you won't get ahead, either.

When farming your business, you plant the seeds by telling people exactly what you do and how you do it. Your business grows because now people know what you offer and start reaching out to you for products and services.

Get to Work!

Start working on the system. Give it a try; we expect you will be amazed at how well this relationship marketing system works.

Quite frankly, if you try this system for 90 days and don't get anything from it, we would be very grateful if you connected with us and said, "This is where I got stuck."

Two things will happen because of your willingness to connect. First, we'll learn something from it and get better, and second, your input will help other folks.

If you find this relationship marketing system works for you, let us know which part of it was most useful! (When you contact us, please put in the email subject line: "Relationship Marketing Book".) We want to celebrate with you. And we ask that you recommend this book to three of your referral partners in the next 90 days. That way, you'll all be on the same page.

We have used this system for years. We have codified and refined it to show others how to use it. Do you understand why we did this? Because it is part of our commitment to be of service to the locally owned business community. After all, we are all in this together and we should work to make all boats rise.

Agreed? Great! Get to it!

We are looking forward to hearing about your massive success. Keep us posted!

Martin Brossman and Pat Howlett
(Martin@MartinBrossman.com)

RESOURCES

We are looking forward to hearing about your massive success from applying this book. Keep us posted! Martin@MartinBrossman.com (919) 847-4757.

Please note that updates about Relationship Marketing[3], will be posted at http://relationshipmarketing3/

Also, make sure to join the Facebook Community at https://www.face book.com/groups/RelationshipMarketing3 or https://bit.ly/rm3faceb ook -- or scan this QR code:

Martin Brossman and Pat Howlett also have produced a self-paced Relationship Marketing training program and here is a link to get 50% off for the $97.00 course: https://bit.ly/rm3studentdiscount

(or scan the following QR code):

The best way to schedule Martin Brossman for success coaching, presentations, speaking engagements, or training sessions is via his assistant, Colleen Gray at Collleen@MartinBrossman.com. Or you can call 919-847-4757 (option #1).

To get in touch with Pat Howlett, go to his website at BeTheGorilla.com or email him directly at Pat@BeTheGorilla.com

Also, if you have written a book or are planning to do so, Martin recommends CedarBooks because it offers premium publishing expertise at affordable prices. To inquire about their consulting, proofreading, editing, illustrating, formatting, launching, and marketing services, please visit CedarBooks.com/publishing

Finally, for excellent editorial service, contact Jane Maulucci at: TheReactiveVoice.com

MARTIN BROSSMAN

Martin Brossman has been helping hundreds of small businesses achieve their goals for decades since he left IBM in 1995. He received the IBM Means Service Award in 11 months, which generally takes 11 years. A real Renaissance man, Martin was awarded "Volunteer of the Year" in September 2000 by former North Carolina governor, James B. Hunt, for his work with cancer patients.

Even in high school, Martin was awarded a National Science Foundation Scholarship in 1977 which inspired him to write a book on how to make holograms. Those achievements were followed, later that year, by an official appointment as an adjunct instructor at his high school to teach a class on Holography to his peers. It is worth noting that those accomplishments occurred despite a childhood diagnosis of dyslexia and ADD.

Decades of men's work, including being one of the co-founders with Pat Howlett of a Raleigh NC JUNTO men's group led, in 2006, to Martin receiving the Ron Herring Mission of Service Award from the Mankind Project for his contributions in helping men. Also in 2006, he began teaching "Marketing for Small Businesses" in community colleges and towns throughout North Carolina — and he continues to do so.

Since 2007, Martin has hosted numerous podcast shows, including a leading social-selling podcast with his late associate, Greg Hyer.

Then, in 2009, Martin pioneered the first social media management certificate program with Anora McGaha and wrote the first book on the topic in the state of NC. Those endeavors eventually led to the creation of a popular course at NC State University called "Social Media Management and Marketing Certificate Program" that has been taught by Martin and his associate Karen Tiede for over a decade. Also, in 2009, he received the Ethel N. Fortner Writer Award, which is the highest literary prize from St. Andrews University.

Martin was born and raised in Washington DC and has lived in Raleigh NC since 1983 with his beautiful bride of many years, Barbara Carr Brossman, near his brilliant stepson, Emery Carr. Martin's hobbies include photography, ham radio (KI4CFS), hiking, meditation, and competition shooting. If you visit Shelley Lake Park in Raleigh, you may find him riding his bicycle, walking, or taking photographs. If you do, don't hesitate to say, "Hi!"

PAT HOWLETT

Pat Howlett is a "localist", family man, husband, father of four, grandpa of seven (and counting), brother, son, and a good neighbor. Fulfilling those roles is the reason he does what he does... his *why*.

Other hats Pat has worn include:

- 40-year small business owner/advocate

- City council member

- Mayor of a small town

- Chamber of Commerce president

- Urban Renewal Authority board member

- Tourism board and river/town clean-up volunteer

- Kiwanis Club president

- Lions Club member

Instrumental to this book's creation is Pat's founding of inside919.com, where he developed the training for *Relationship Marketing*[3], met Martin Brossman, and together began the journey of directly helping micro businesses succeed. All of these pursuits represented opportunities for Pat to create lifelong relationships, which is unsurprising because, as he and Martin frequently point out, life's most important activities generally do involve *relationships*.

Although this book focuses on how you can reach your business goals via relationship marketing, Pat encourages you to not stop here, "Once you understand *Relationship Marketing*[3], share it with three others!"